MAZE

FOR KIDS

MAZE BOOK

 /MySweetBooks1

 /MySweetBooks1

 /MySweetBooks1

 /MySweetBooks

Email Us : mysweetbooks1@gmail.com

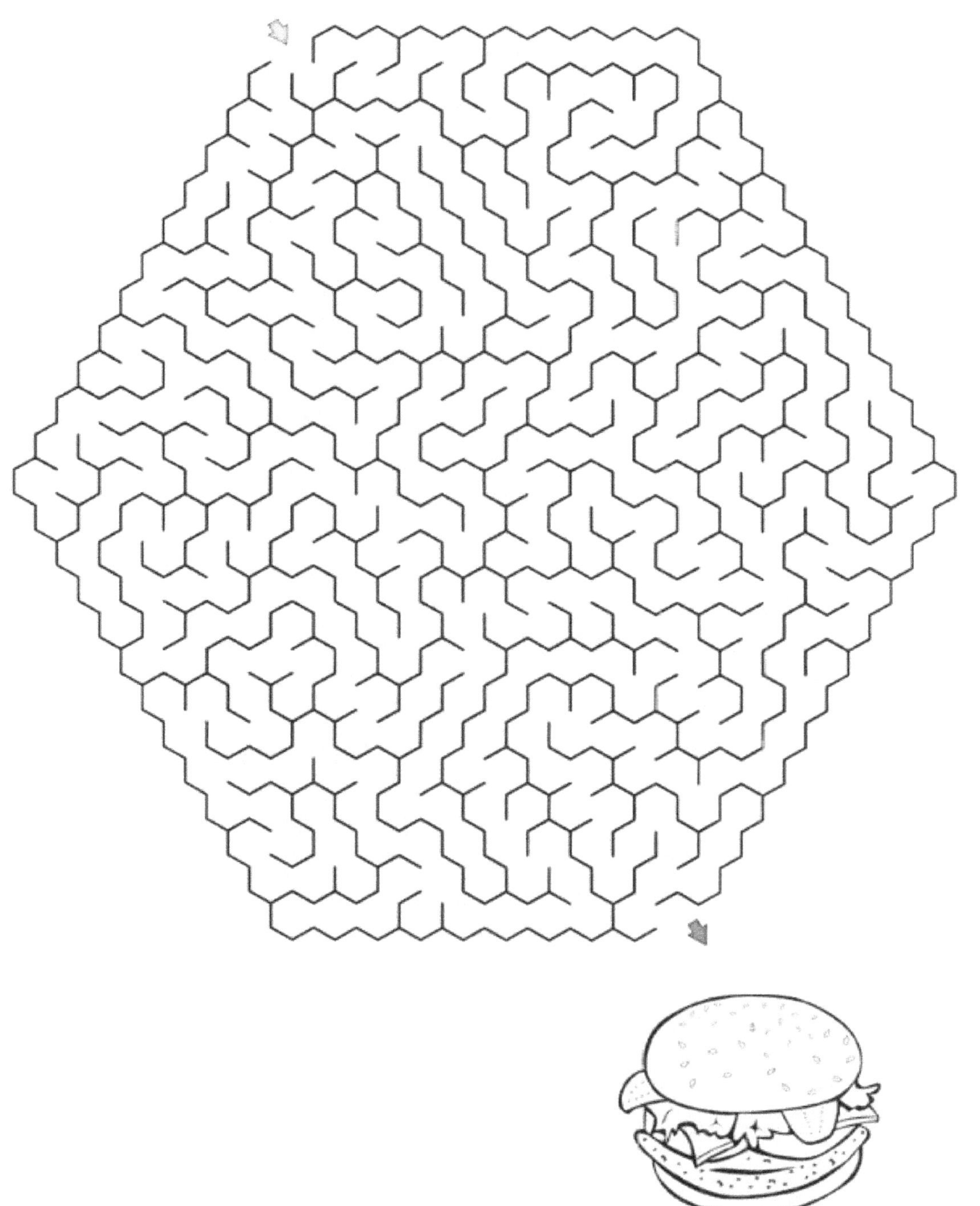

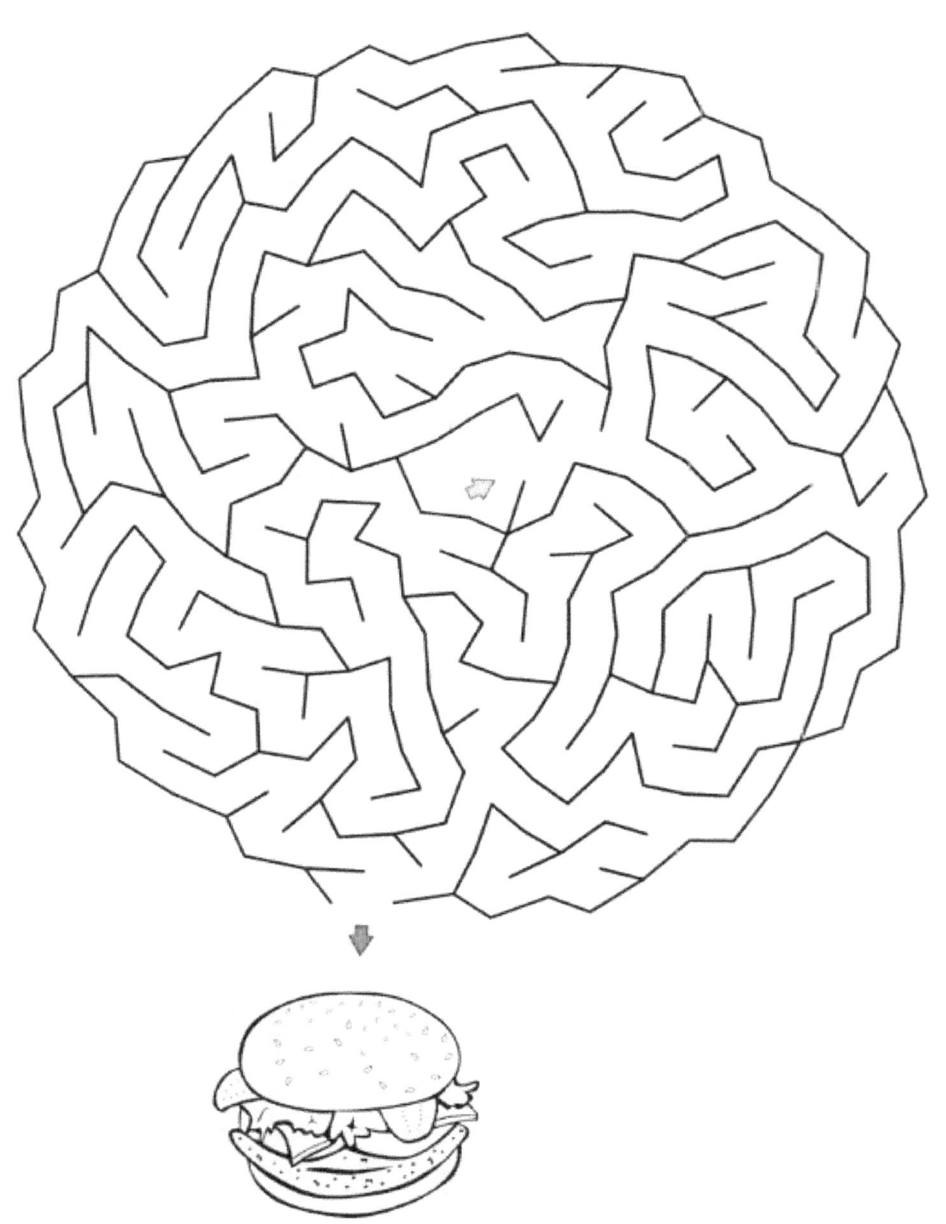

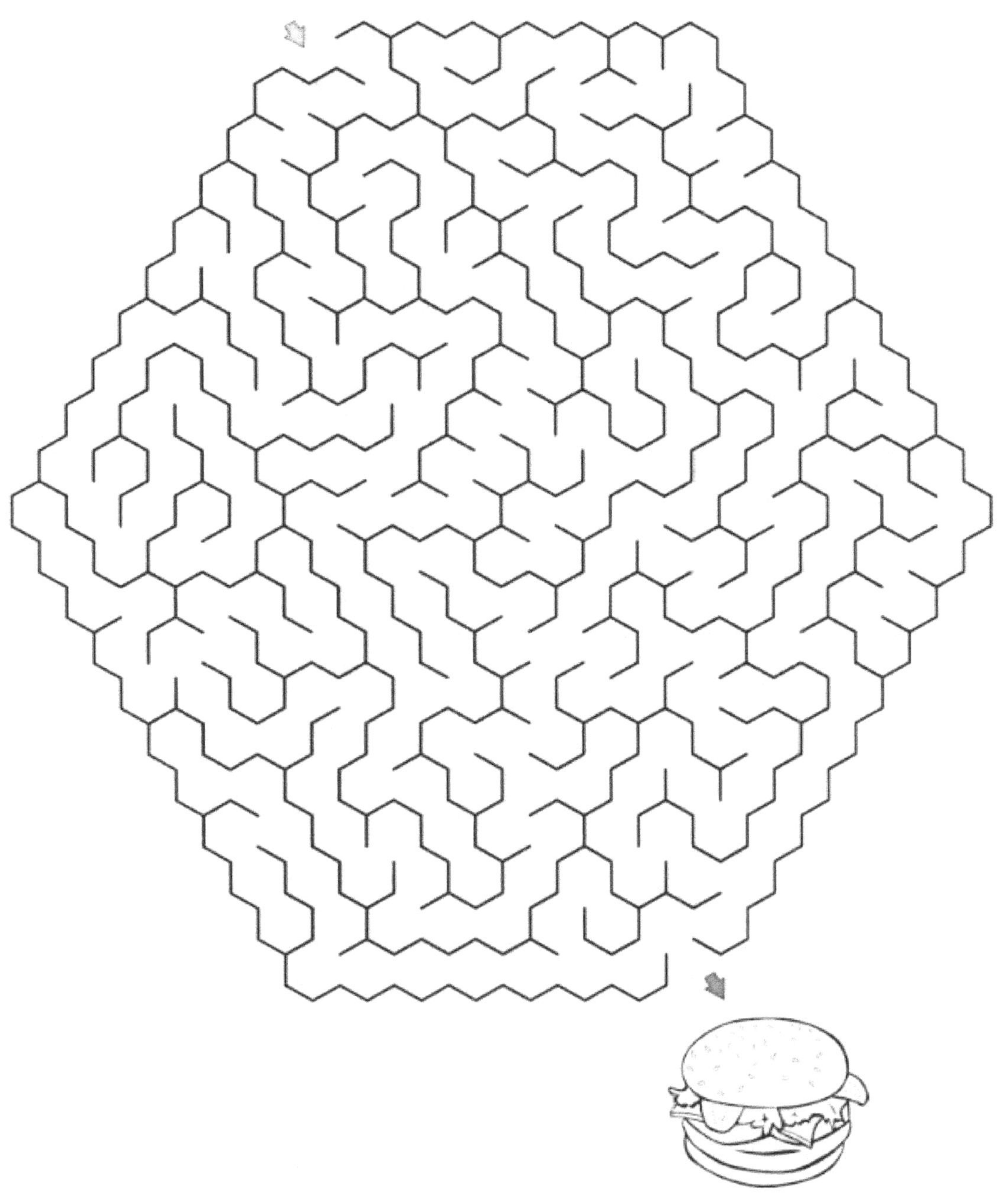

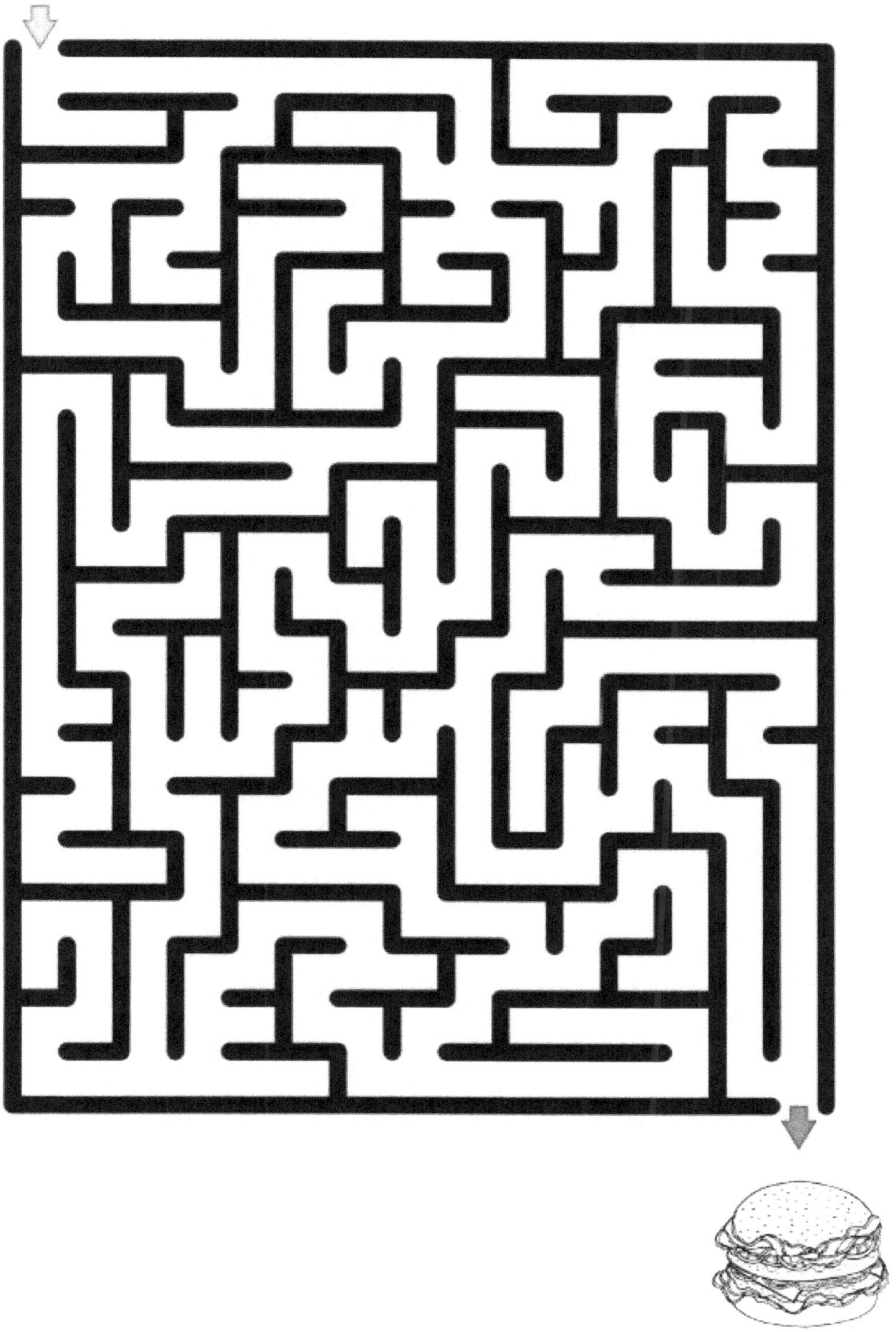

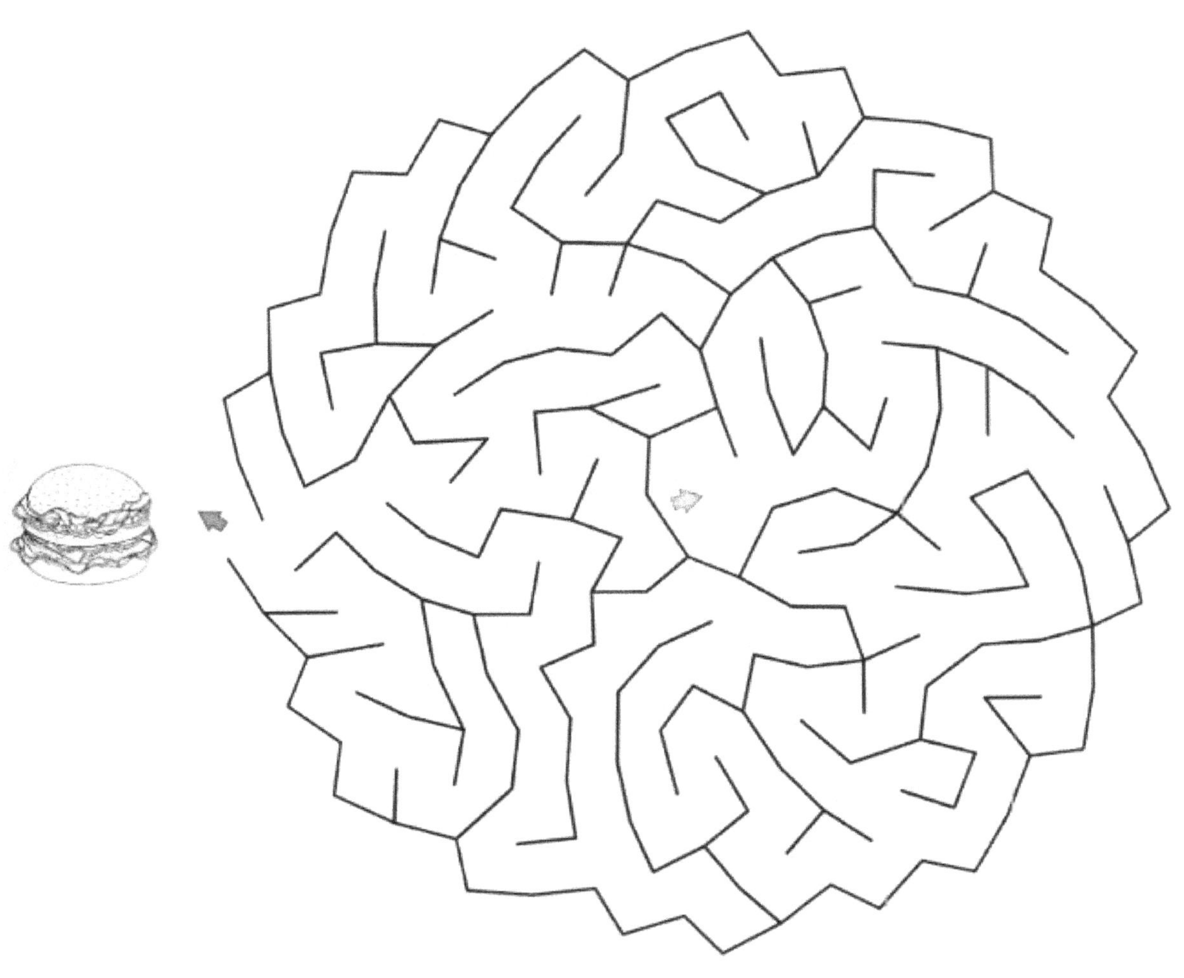

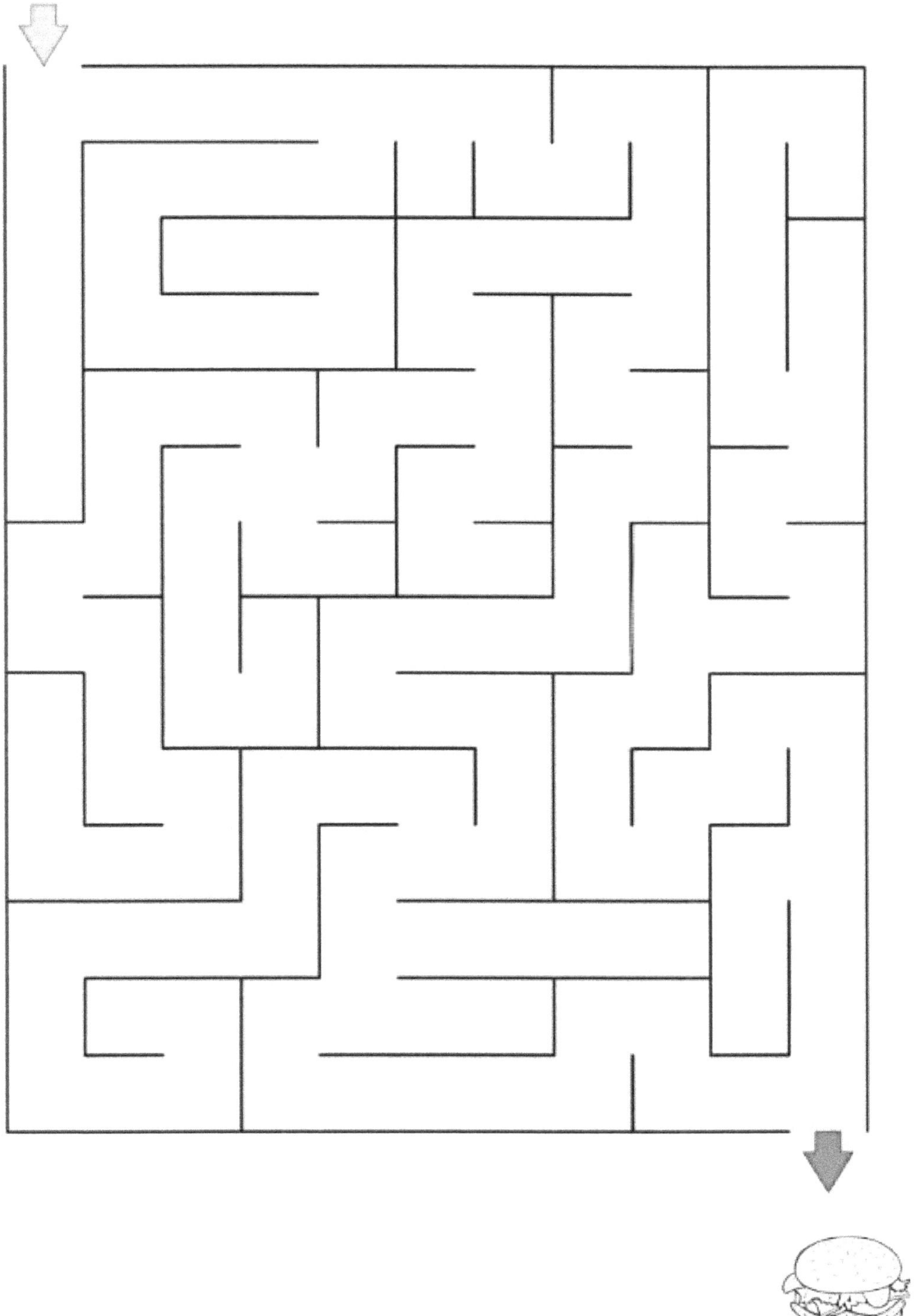

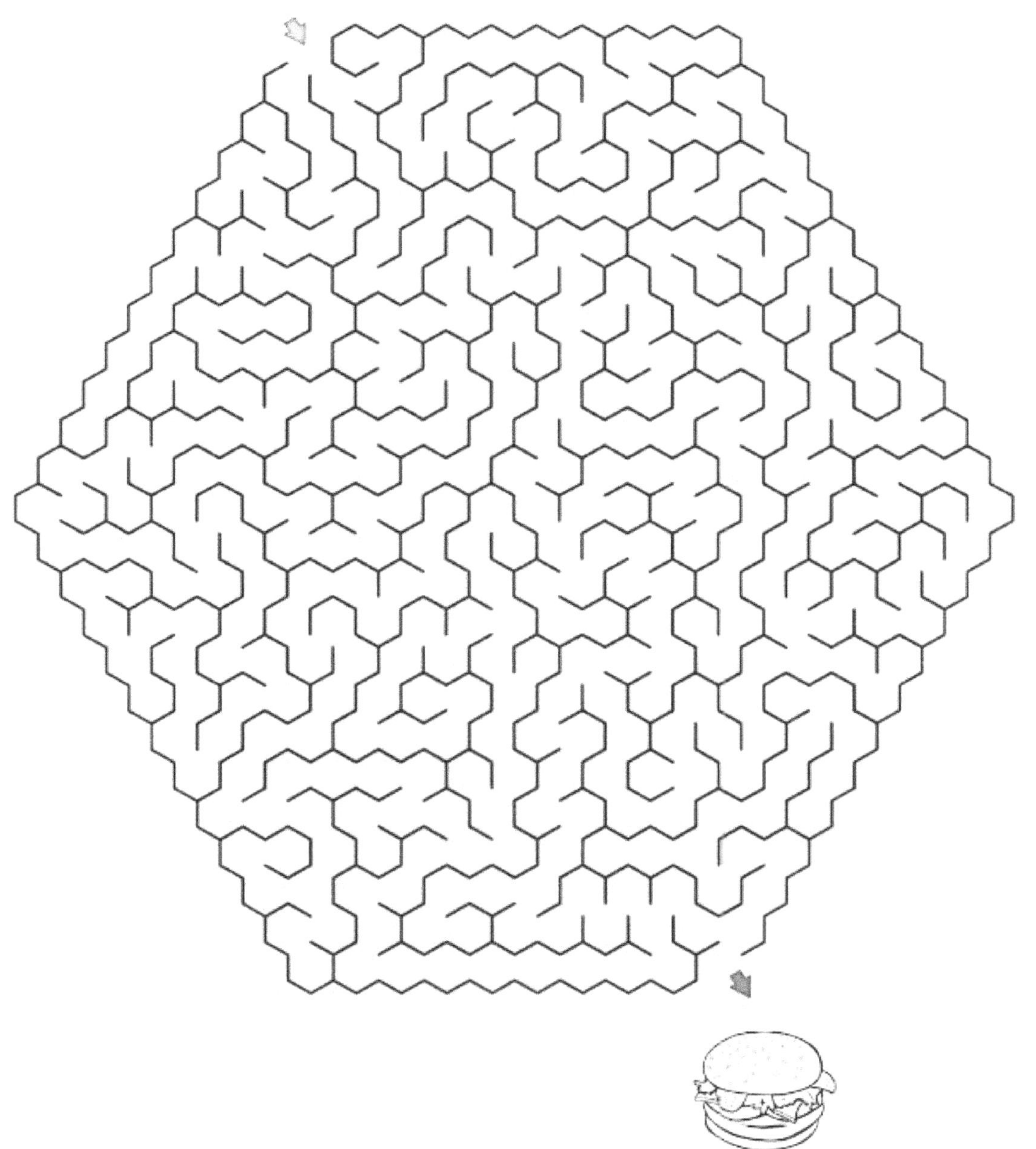

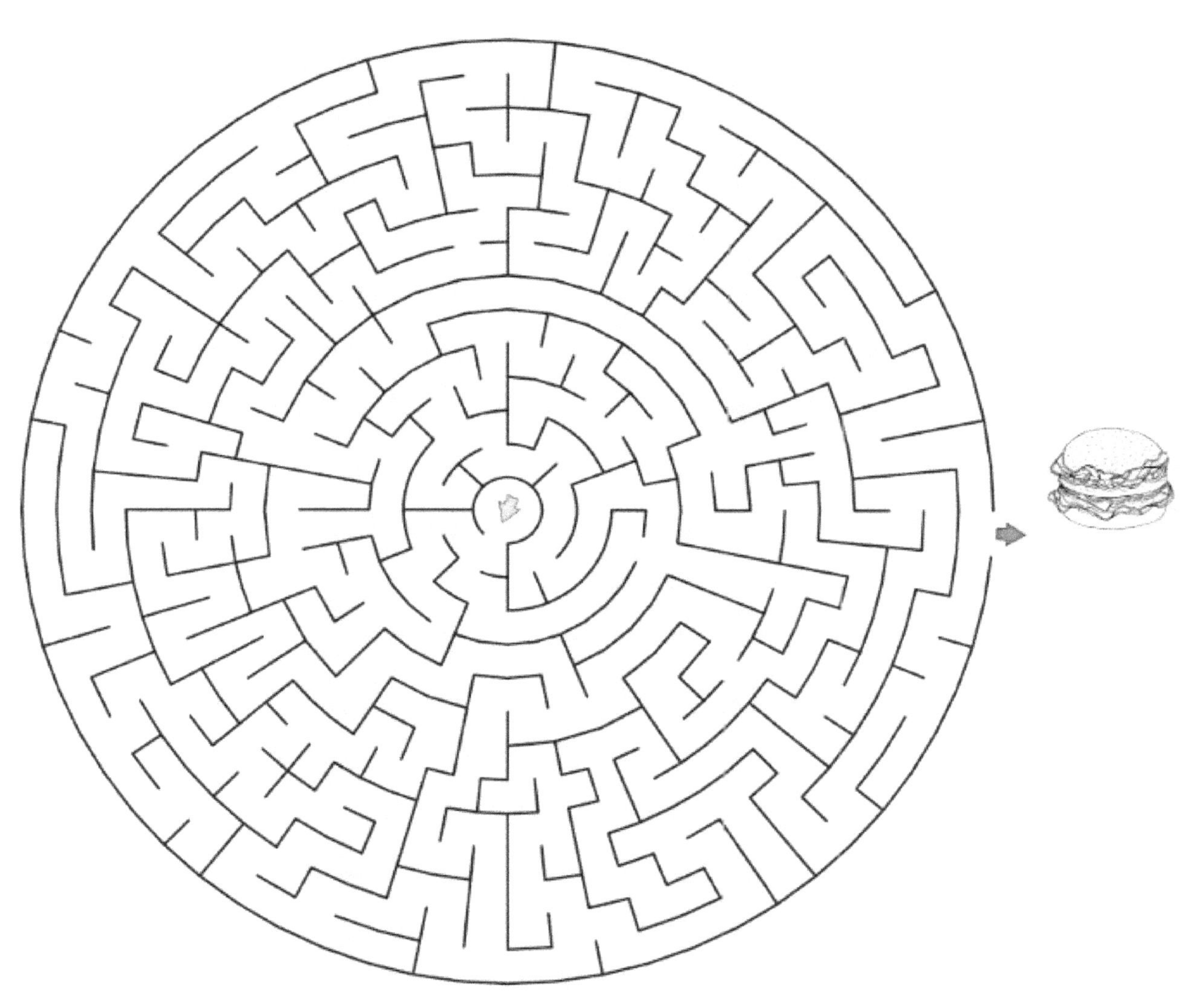

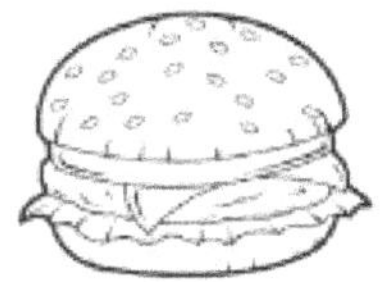

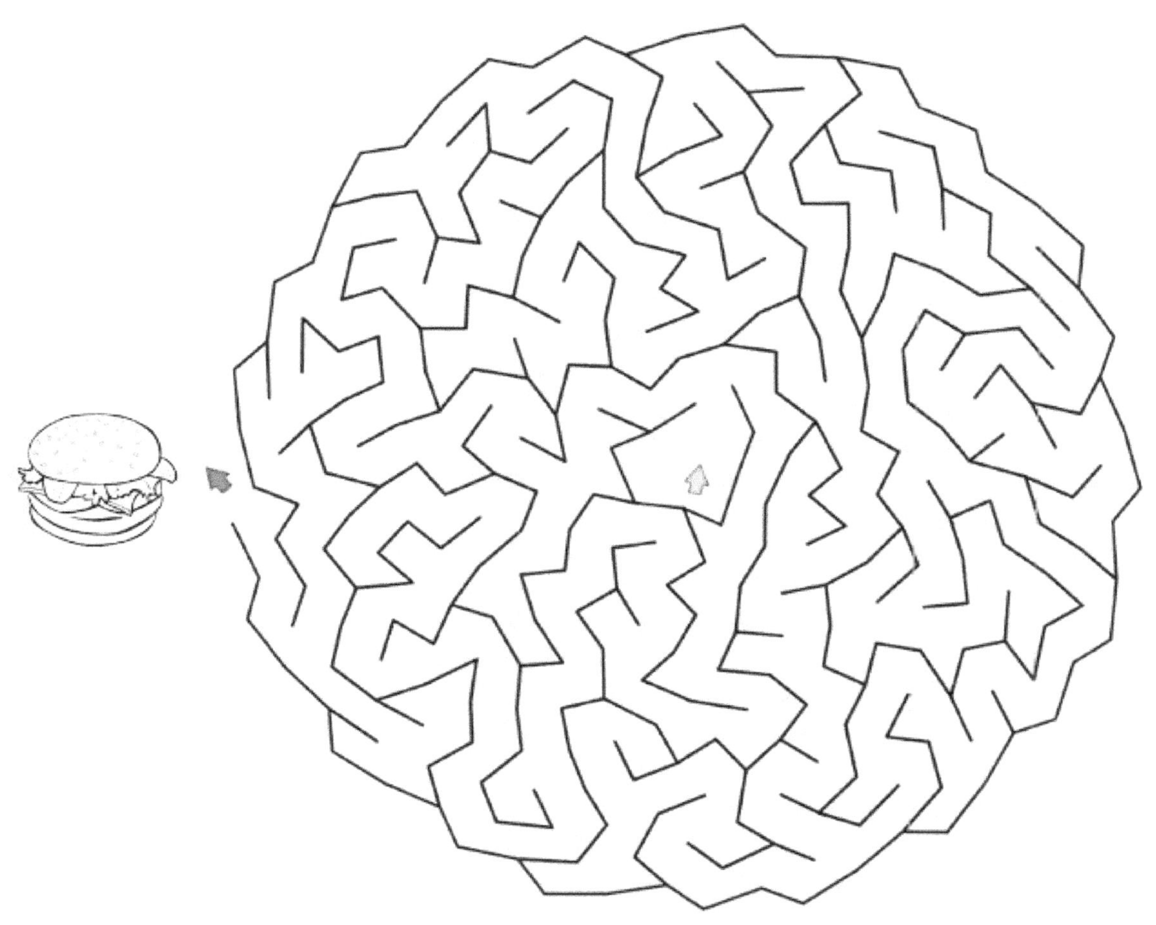

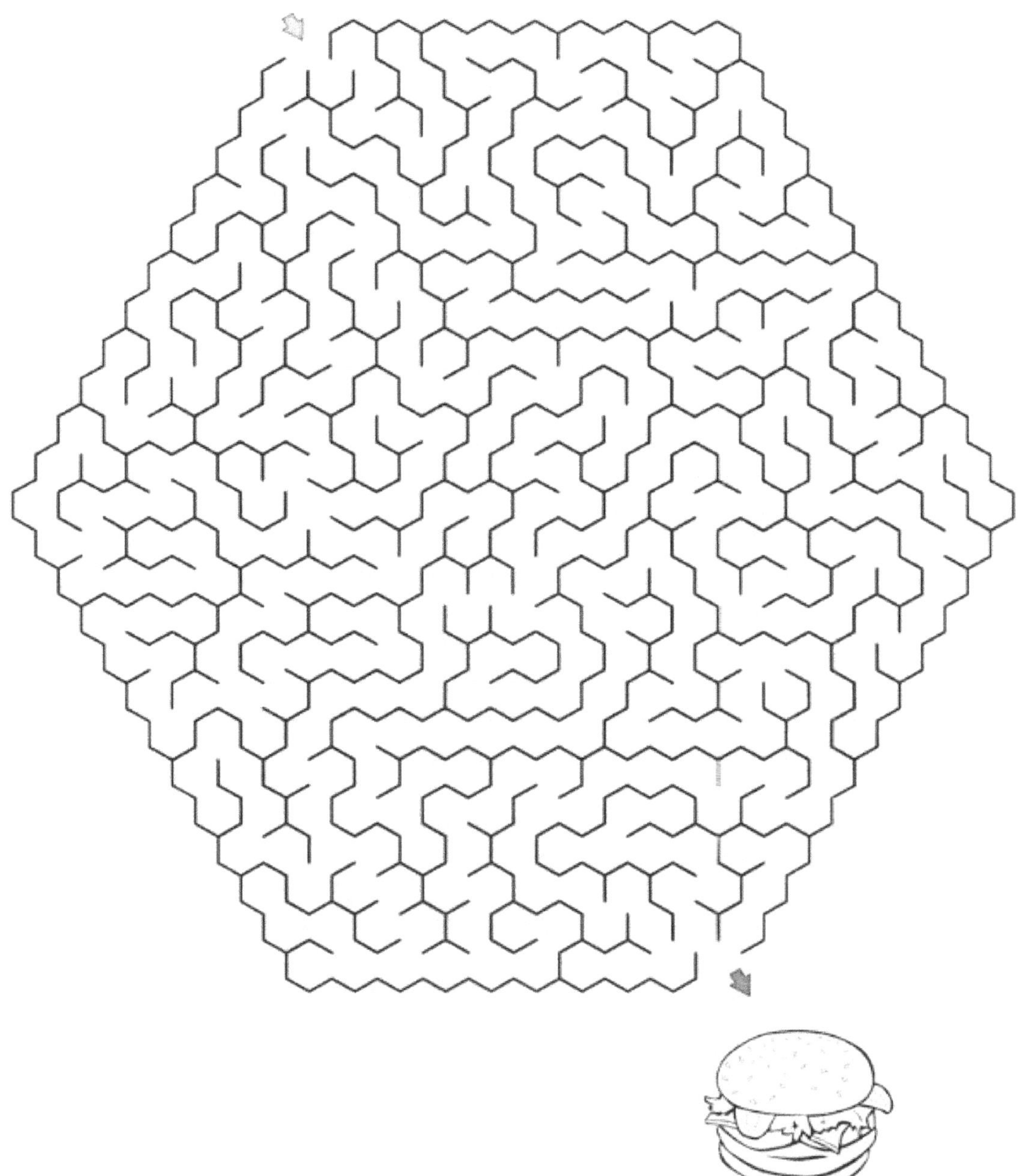

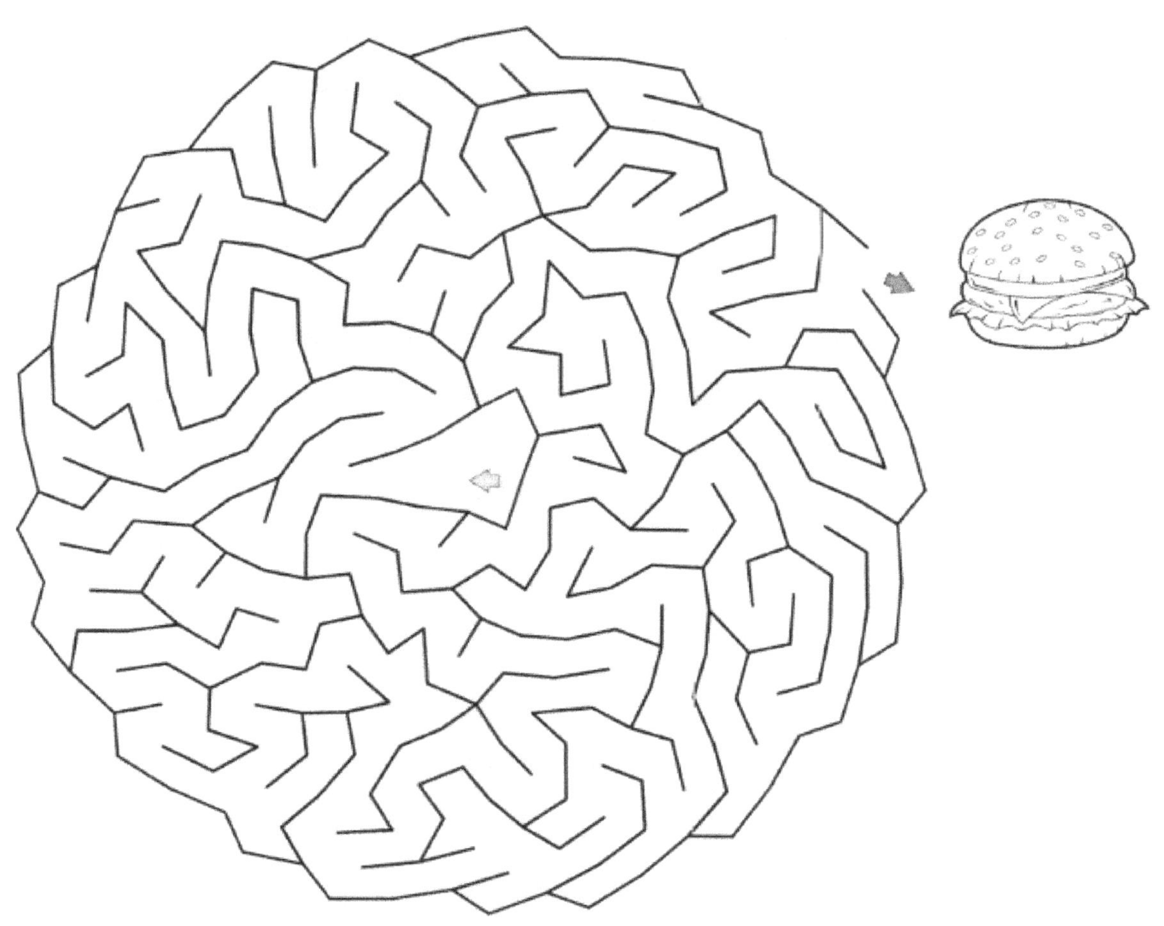

www.ingramcontent.com/pod-product-compliance
Lightning Source LLC
Chambersburg PA
CBHW081737250726
48657CB00010B/3307